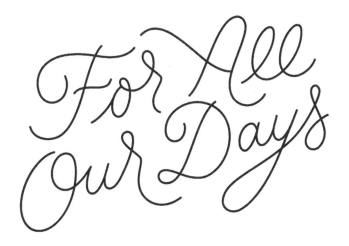

Library of Congress Cataloging-in-Publication Data

Names: Farrugia, Mallory, editor.
Title: For all our days : a collection of wedding readings / [edited by] Mallory Farrugia.
Description: San Francisco : Chronicle Books, [2020] | Includes bibliographical references. | Summary: "With an elegant and timeless package, this collection of readings is a must-have for any couple planning their wedding. The readings range from the romantic, traditional, and religious - such as Shakespearean sonnets, biblical verses, or passages from the Qu'ran - to the modern, fresh, and humorous - such as popular song lyrics, the Supreme Court ruling on gay marriage, or an excerpt from a stand-up comedy routine - ensuring that there's something that appeals to everyone. Engaged couples will enjoy perusing these pages in search of the perfect reading, and the thoroughly romantic presentation - with a textural, foil-stamped cover and satin bookmark - makes this anthology a lovely keepsake for newlyweds long after their wedding is over"— Provided by publisher.
Identifiers: LCCN 2019027715 | ISBN 9781452182377 (hardcover) | ISBN 9781452182407 (ebook)
Subjects: LCSH: Weddings—Literary collections. | Marriage—Literary collections. | Love—Literary collections. | Marriage customs and rites.
Classification: LCC PN6071.W4 F67 2020 | DDC 808.8/03543—dc23
LC record available at https://lccn.loc.gov/2019027715

Manufactured in China.

Licensing by Mallory Farrugia.

Art by Channin Fulton.

Design by Katherine Yao.

10 9 8 7 6 5 4 3 2 1

Chronicle books and gifts are available at special quantity discounts to corporations, professional associations, literacy programs, and other organizations. For details and discount information, please contact our premiums department at corporatesales@chroniclebooks.com or at 1-800-759-0190.

Chronicle Books LLC
680 Second Street
San Francisco, CA 94107

www.chroniclebooks.com

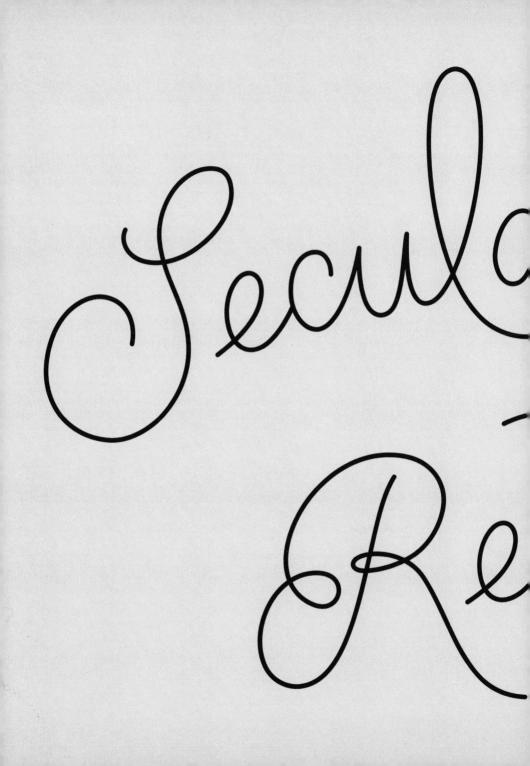

INTRODUCTION

In these pages, you'll find a collection of inspiring readings, insightful musings, and sage advice on love and marriage. They range from the traditional, romantic, and religious, to the modern, quirky, and humorous; from Native American blessings and Shakespearean sonnets, to excerpts from novels, love letters, and comedy routines. With such an assortment, our hope is that you will find something in this book—whether you choose to use it at your wedding or not—that embodies a little bit of what love means to you and your partner.

While this is a thorough and diverse compilation of readings, there are, of course, plenty of other options to consider when planning your ceremony. Think about your favorite songs, movies, or books. Are there lyrics that speak to you, quotes that resonate, or excerpts that define what marriage means to you? Perhaps there is a sentimental section in your favorite picture book, or a meaningful passage from a famous speech. Consider religious or cultural references, as well. How can you honor your heritage or incorporate your and your partner's spiritual beliefs? Or, perhaps you have a friend who is an excellent poet or songwriter who can craft something unique to read or sing. Bottom line, your ceremony should reflect who you are, both together and separately.

Your wedding ceremony also marks the beginning of your married life, so take this opportunity to define what you want your marriage to look like. How do you envision your life together? What are your values and priorities? What promises do you intend to keep? Your readings and vows can be a wonderful way to communicate those things to each other and to your community.

During the ceremony itself, make sure to pause, take a breath, and soak it all in. And don't forget to enjoy it. It's not every day that you get to declare your love in front of family and friends—and then eat, drink, and dance the night away! Remember that your wedding is a celebration of the two of you and your love for each other—and that's the most important thing.

As the months and years go by, we hope you'll turn back to this little collection of words and wisdom as a reminder of what love is all about.

TABLE OF CONTENTS

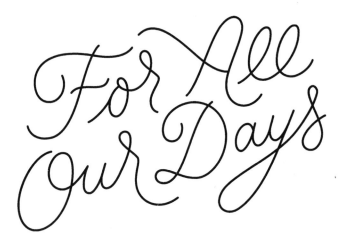

For All Our Days

A COLLECTION *of* WEDDING READINGS

CHRONICLE BOOKS

SAN FRANCISCO

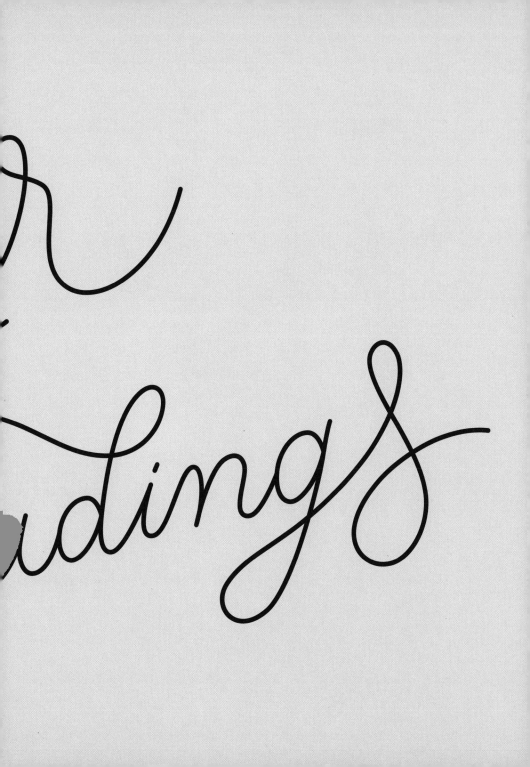

SONNET 116

1609 / WILLIAM SHAKESPEARE

Let me not to the marriage of true minds
Admit impediments. Love is not love
Which alters when it alteration finds,
Or bends with the remover to remove:
O, no! it is an ever-fixed mark,
That looks on tempests and is never shaken;
It is the star to every wandering bark,
Whose worth's unknown, although his height be taken.
Love's not Time's fool, though rosy lips and cheeks
Within his bending sickle's compass come;
Love alters not with his brief hours and weeks,
But bears it out even to the edge of doom.
      If this be error and upon me proved,
      I never writ, nor no man ever loved.

THE GOOD-MORROW
from SONGS AND SONNETS

1635–69 / JOHN DONNE

I wonder by my troth, what thou, and I
Did, till we loved? were we not weaned till then?
But sucked on country pleasures, childishly?
Or snorted we in the seven sleepers den?
'Twas so; But this, all pleasures fancies be.
If ever any beauty I did see,
Which I desired, and got, 'twas but a dream of thee.

And now good-morrow to our waking souls,
Which watch not one another out of fear;
For love, all love of other sights controls,
And makes one little room, an everywhere.
Let sea-discoverers to new worlds have gone,
Let Maps to other, worlds on worlds have shown,
Let us possess one world, each hath one, and is one.

My face in thine eye, thine in mine appears,
And true plain hearts do in the faces rest,
Where can we find two better hemispheres
Without sharp North, without declining West?
Whatever dies, was not mixt equally;
If our two loves be one, or, thou and I
Love so alike, that none do slacken, none can die.

From

PARADISE LOST

1667 / JOHN MILTON

With thee conversing I forget all time,
All seasons and their change, all please alike.
Sweet is the breath of Morn, her rising sweet,
With charm of earliest birds; pleasant the Sun
When first on this delightful land he spreads
His orient beams, on herb, tree, fruit, and flour,
Glistening with dew; fragrant the fertile earth
After soft showers; and sweet the coming on
Of grateful evening mild, then silent Night
With this her solemn bird and this fair Moon,
And these the gems of Heaven, her starry train:
But neither breath of Morn when she ascends
With charm of earliest birds, nor rising Sun
On this delightful land, nor herb, fruit, flower,
Glistening with dew, nor fragrance after showers,
Nor grateful Evening mild, nor silent night
With this her solemn bird, nor walk by Moon,
Or glittering starlight without thee is sweet.

TO MY DEAR AND LOVING HUSBAND

1678 / ANNE BRADSTREET

If ever two were one then surely we.
If ever man were loved by wife, then thee;
If ever wife was happy in a man,
Compare with me ye women if you can.
I prize thy love more than whole mines of gold,
Or all the riches that the East doth hold.
My love is such that rivers cannot quench,
Nor aught but love from thee give recompense.
Thy love is such I can no way repay,
The heavens reward thee, manifold I pray.
Then while we live, in love let's so persever,
That when we live no more, we may live ever.

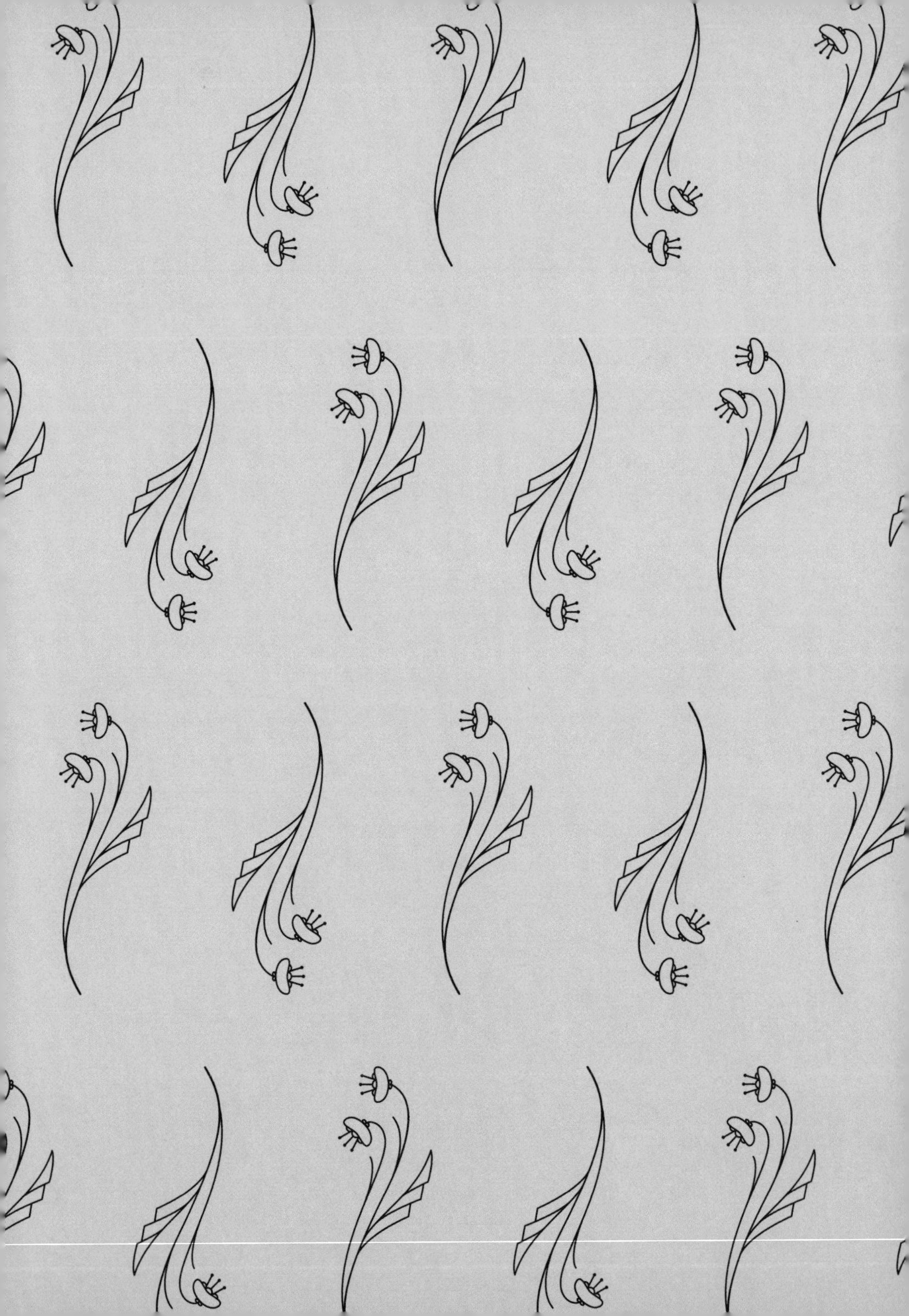

From
A LOVE LETTER

DECEMBER 23, 1782 / ABIGAIL ADAMS TO
JOHN ADAMS

My dearest Friend,

. . . Should I draw you the picture of my heart, it
would be what I hope you still would love, though
it contained nothing new. The early possession you
obtained there, and the absolute power you have
ever maintained over it, leave not the smallest
space unoccupied. I look back to the early days of
our acquaintance and friendship, as to the days
of love and innocence, and with an indescribable
pleasure I have seen near a score of years roll
over our heads, with an affection heightened and
improved by time; nor have the dreary years of
absence in the smallest degree effaced from my
mind the image of the dear, untitled man to whom
I gave my heart.

From
A RED, RED ROSE

1794 / ROBERT BURNS

O my Love is like a red, red rose
   That's newly sprung in June;
O my Love is like the melody
   That's sweetly played in tune.

So fair art thou, my bonnie lass,
   So deep in love am I;
And I will love thee still, my dear,
   Till all the seas gang dry.

Till all the seas gang dry, my dear,
   And the rocks melt with the sun;
I will love thee still, my dear,
   While the sands of life shall run.

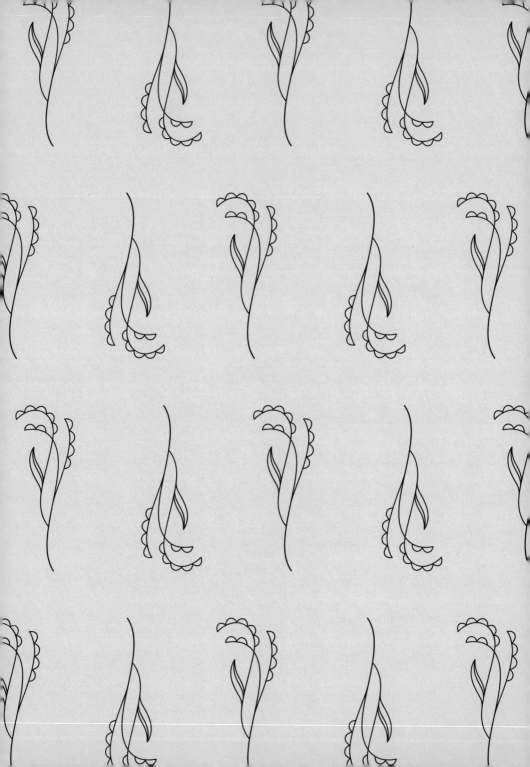

LOVE'S PHILOSOPHY

1819 / PERCY BYSSHE SHELLEY

1 /

The fountains mingle with the river
And the rivers with the Ocean,
The winds of Heaven mix forever
With a sweet emotion;
Nothing in the world is single;
All things by a law divine
In one spirit meet and mingle.
Why not I with thine?—

2 /

See the mountains kiss high Heaven
And the waves clasp one another;
No sister-flower would be forgiven
If it disdained its brother;
And the sunlight clasps the earth
And the moonbeams kiss the sea:
What is all this sweet work worth
If thou kiss not me?

From
JANE EYRE

1847 / CHARLOTTE BRONTË

Mr. Rochester to Jane:

"You see now how the case stands—do you not?" he
continued. "After a youth and manhood passed half
in unutterable misery and half in dreary solitude, I
have for the first time found what I can truly love—I
have found you. You are my sympathy—my better
self—my good angel. I am bound to you with a strong
attachment. I think you good, gifted, lovely: a fervent,
a solemn passion is conceived in my heart; it leans to
you, draws you to my centre and spring of life, wraps
my existence about you, and, kindling in pure, powerful
flame, fuses you and me in one."

From
SONNETS FROM THE PORTUGUESE

———————

1850 / ELIZABETH BARRETT BROWNING

43 /

How do I love thee? Let me count the ways.
I love thee to the depth and breadth and height
My soul can reach, when feeling out of sight
For the ends of Being and ideal Grace.
I love thee to the level of everyday's
Most quiet need, by sun and candlelight.
I love thee freely, as men strive for Right;
I love thee purely, as they turn from Praise.
I love thee with the passion put to use
In my old griefs, and with my childhood's faith.
I love thee with a love I seemed to lose
With my lost saints,—I love thee with the breath,
Smiles, tears, of all my life!—and, if God choose,
I shall but love thee better after death.

From

SONG OF THE OPEN ROAD
in LEAVES OF GRASS

1855 / WALT WHITMAN

1 /

Afoot and light-hearted I take to the open road,

Healthy, free, the world before me,

The long brown path before me leading wherever I choose.

. . .

11 /

Listen! I will be honest with you,

I do not offer the old smooth prizes, but offer rough new
prizes,

These are the days that must happen to you:

You shall not heap up what is called riches,

You shall scatter with lavish hand all that you earn or achieve

. . .

15 /

. . .

Camerado, I give you my hand!

I give you my love more precious than money,

I give you myself before preaching or law;

Will you give me yourself? will you come travel with me?

Shall we stick by each other as long as we live?

From
ADAM BEDE

1859 / GEORGE ELIOT

But this second time she looked round. What a look of yearning love it was that the mild grey eyes turned on the strong dark-eyed man! She did not start again at the sight of him; she said nothing, but moved towards him so that his arm could clasp her round.

And they walked on so in silence, while the warm tears fell. Adam was content, and said nothing. It was Dinah who spoke first.

"Adam," she said, "it is the Divine Will. My soul is so knit to yours that it is but a divided life I live without you. And this moment, now you are with me, and I feel that our hearts are filled with the same love. I have a fulness of strength to bear and do our heavenly Father's Will that I had lost before."

Adam paused and looked into her sincere eyes.

"Then we'll never part any more, Dinah, till death parts us."

And they kissed each other with a deep joy.

What greater thing is there for two human souls than to feel that they are joined for life—to strengthen each other in all labour, to rest on each other in all sorrow, to minister to each other in all pain, to be one with each other in silent unspeakable memories at the moment of the last parting?

From
LES MISÉRABLES

1862 / VICTOR HUGO

The future belongs to hearts even more than it does to minds. Love, that is the only thing that can occupy and fill eternity. In the infinite, the inexhaustible is requisite.

Love participates of the soul itself. It is of the same nature. Like it, it is the divine spark; like it, it is incorruptible, indivisible, imperishable. It is a point of fire that exists within us, which is immortal and infinite, which nothing can confine, and which nothing can extinguish. We feel it burning even to the very marrow of our bones, and we see it beaming in the very depths of heaven . . .

You look at a star for two reasons, because it is luminous, and because it is impenetrable. You have beside you a sweeter radiance and a greater mystery, woman . . .

When love has fused and mingled two beings in a sacred and angelic unity, the secret of life has been discovered so far as they are concerned; they are no longer anything more than the two boundaries of the same destiny; they are no longer anything but the two wings of the same spirit. Love, soar . . .

What a grand thing it is to be loved! What a far grander thing it is to love! The heart becomes heroic, by dint of passion. It is no longer composed of anything but what is pure; it no longer rests on anything that is not elevated and great. An unworthy thought can no more germinate in it, than a nettle on a glacier. The serene and lofty soul, inaccessible to vulgar passions and emotions, dominating the clouds and the shades of this world, its follies, its lies, its hatreds, its vanities, its miseries, inhabits the blue of heaven, and no longer feels anything but profound and subterranean shocks of destiny, as the crests of mountains feel the shocks of earthquake.

THE OWL AND THE PUSSY-CAT from NONSENSE SONGS, STORIES, BOTANY, AND ALPHABETS

1871 / EDWARD LEAR

I /

The Owl and the Pussy-Cat went to sea
   In a beautiful pea-green boat:
They took some honey, and plenty of money
   Wrapped up in a five-pound note.
The Owl looked up to the stars above,
   And sang to a small guitar,
"O lovely Pussy, O Pussy, my love,
   What a beautiful Pussy you are,
     You are,
     You are!
   What a beautiful Pussy you are!"

II /

Pussy said to the Owl, "You elegant fowl,
   How charmingly sweet you sing!
Oh! let us be married; too long we have tarried:
   But what shall we do for a ring?"

They sailed away, for a year and a day,
  To the land where the bong-tree grows;
And there in a wood a Piggy-wig stood,
  With a ring at the end of his nose,
    His nose,
    His nose,
  With a ring at the end of his nose.

III /

"Dear Pig, are you willing to sell for one shilling
  Your ring?" Said the Piggy, "I will."
So they took it away, and were married next day
  By the Turkey who lives on the hill.
They dined on mince and slices of quince,
  Which they ate with a runcible spoon;
And hand in hand, on the edge of the sand,
  They danced by the light of the moon,
    The moon,
    The moon,
  They danced by the light of the moon.

MONNA INNOMINATA

———

1876 / CHRISTINA ROSSETTI

4 /

I loved you first: but afterwards your love
    Outsoaring mine, sang such a loftier song
As drowned the friendly cooings of my dove.
    Which owes the other most? my love was long,
    And yours one moment seemed to wax more strong;
I loved and guessed at you, you construed me
And loved me for what might or might not be—
    Nay, weights and measures do us both a wrong.
For verily love knows not "mine" or "thine;"
    With separate "I" and "thou" free love has done,
        For one is both and both are one in love:
Rich love knows nought of "thine that is not mine;"
        Both have the strength and both the length thereof,
    Both of us of the love which makes us one.

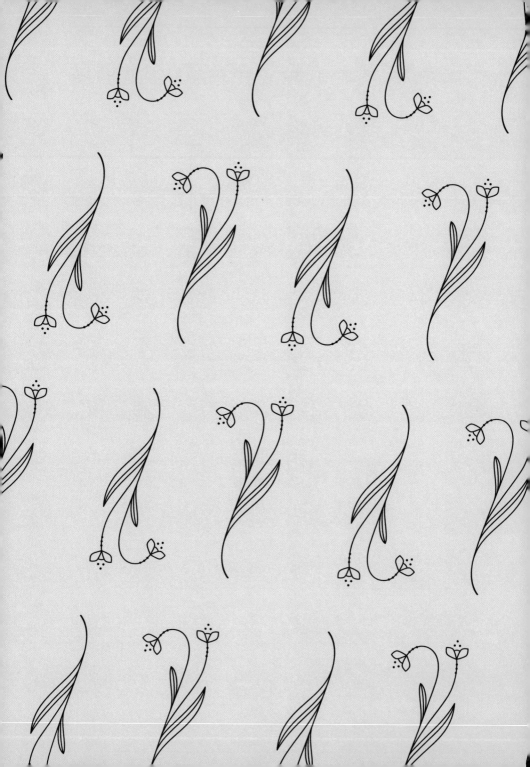

From

PORTRAIT OF A LADY

1881 / HENRY JAMES

Gilbert Osmond to Isabel Archer:

"It has made me better, loving you," he said on
another occasion; "it has made me wiser and
easier and—I won't pretend to deny—brighter and
nicer and even stronger. I used to want a great
many things before and to be angry I didn't have
them. Theoretically I was satisfied, as I once told
you. I flattered myself I had limited my wants.
But I was subject to irritation; I used to have
morbid, sterile, hateful fits of hunger, of desire.
Now I'm really satisfied, because I can't think
of anything better."

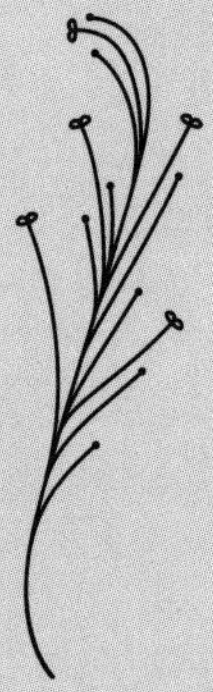

From
POEMS:
THIRD SERIES

———————

1896 / EMILY DICKINSON

26 /

It's all I have to bring to-day,
    This, and my heart beside,
This, and my heart, and all the fields,
    And all the meadows wide.
Be sure you count, should I forget, —
    Someone the sum could tell, —
This, and my heart, and all the bees
    Which in the clover dwell.

THE ART OF MARRIAGE
from THE ART OF LIVING

1961 / WILFERD A. PETERSON

Happiness in marriage is not something that just happens. A good marriage must be created. In the art of marriage the *little things* are the *big things* . . .

It is never being too old to hold hands.

It is remembering to say "I love you," at least once each day.

It is never going to sleep angry.

It is at no time taking the other for granted; the courtship shouldn't end with the honeymoon, it should continue through all the years.

It is having a mutual sense of values and common objectives; it is standing together facing the world.

It is forming a circle of love that gathers in the whole family.

It is doing things for each other, not in the attitude of duty or sacrifice, but in the spirit of joy.

It is speaking words of appreciation and demonstrating gratitude in thoughtful ways.

It is not expecting the husband to wear a halo or the wife to have wings of an angel. It is not looking for perfection in each other. It is cultivating flexibility, patience, understanding and a sense of humor.

It is having the capacity to forgive and forget.

It is giving each other an atmosphere in which each can grow.

It is finding room for the things of the spirit. It is a common search for the good and the beautiful.

It is not only marrying the right partner, it is *being* the right partner.

It is discovering what marriage can be, at its best, as expressed in the words Mark Twain used in a tribute to his wife: "Wherever she was, there was Eden."

From
THE VELVETEEN RABBIT

———————

1922 / MARGERY WILLIAMS

"What is REAL?" asked the Rabbit one day, when they were lying side by side near the nursery fender, before Nana came to tidy the room. "Does it mean having things that buzz inside you and a stick-out handle?"

"Real isn't how you are made," said the Skin Horse. "It's a thing that happens to you. When a child loves you for a long, long time, not just to play with, but REALLY loves you, then you become Real."

"Does it hurt?" asked the Rabbit.

"Sometimes," said the Skin Horse, for he was always truthful. "When you are Real you don't mind being hurt."

"Does it happen all at once, like being wound up," he asked, "or bit by bit?"

"It doesn't happen all at once," said the Skin Horse. "You become. It takes a long time. That's why it doesn't happen often to people who break easily, or have sharp edges, or who have to be carefully kept. Generally, by the time you are Real, most of your hair has been loved off, and your eyes drop out and you get loose in the joints and very shabby. But these things don't matter at all, because once you are Real you can't be ugly, except to people who don't understand."

From

THE PROPHET

1923 / KAHLIL GIBRAN

You were born together, and together you shall be forevermore.

You shall be together when the white wings of death scatter your days.

Aye, you shall be together even in the silent memory of God.

But let there be spaces in your togetherness,

And let the winds of the heavens dance between you.

Love one another, but make not a bond of love:

Let it rather be a moving sea between the shores of your souls.

Fill each other's cup but drink not from one cup.

Give one another of your bread but eat not from the same loaf. Sing and dance together and be joyous, but let each one of you be alone,

Even as the strings of a lute are alone though they quiver with the same music.

Give your hearts, but not into each other's keeping.

For only the hand of Life can contain your hearts.

And stand together yet not too near together:

For the pillars of the temple stand apart,

And the oak tree and the cypress grow not in each other's shadow.

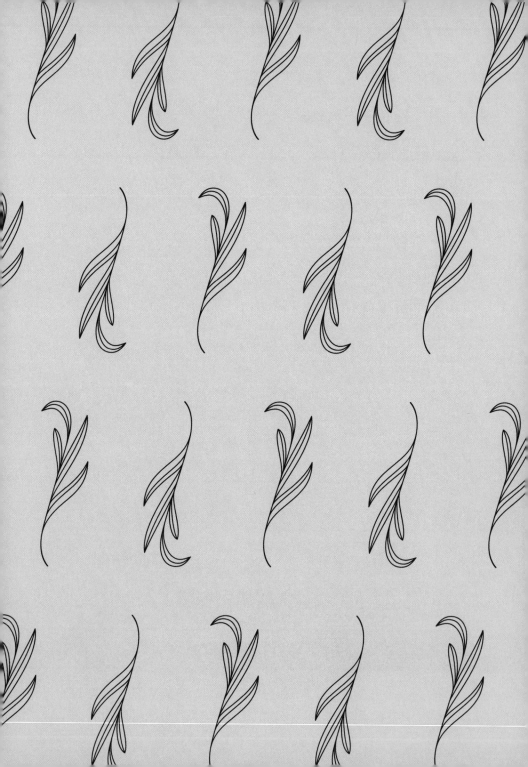

From
LETTERS TO A YOUNG POET

1934 / RAINER MARIA RILKE,
TRANSLATED BY M. D. HERTER NORTON

Marriage is in many ways a simplification of life, and it naturally combines the strengths and wills of two young people so that, together, they seem to reach farther into the future than they did before. Above all, marriage is a new task and a new seriousness,—a new demand on the strength and generosity of each partner, and a great new danger for both.

The point of marriage is not to create a quick commonality by tearing down all boundaries; on the contrary, a good marriage is one in which each partner appoints the other to be the guardian of their solitude, and thus they show each other the greatest possible trust. A merging of two people is an impossibility, and where it seems to exist, it is a hemming-in, a mutual consent that robs one party or both parties of their fullest freedom and development. But once the realization is accepted that even between the closest people infinite distances exist, a marvelous living side by side can grow up for them, if they succeed in loving the expanse between them, which gives them the possibility of always seeing each other as a whole and before an immense sky.

[I CARRY YOUR HEART WITH ME(I CARRY IT IN]

1952 / E.E. CUMMINGS

i carry your heart with me(i carry it in
my heart)i am never without it(anywhere
i go you go,my dear;and whatever is done
by only me is your doing,my darling)
                              i fear
no fate(for you are my fate,my sweet)i want
no world(for beautiful you are my world,my true)
and it's you are whatever a moon has always meant
and whatever a sun will always sing is you

here is the deepest secret nobody knows
(here is the root of the root and the bud of the bud
and the sky of the sky of a tree called life;which grows
higher than the soul can hope or mind can hide)
and this is the wonder that's keeping the stars apart

i carry your heart(i carry it in my heart)

SONNET XVII
from 100 LOVE SONNETS

1959 / PABLO NERUDA
TRANSLATED BY STEPHEN TAPSCOTT (1986)

I do not love you as if you were salt-rose, or topaz,
or the arrow of the carnations the fire shoots off.
I love you as certain dark things are to be loved,
in secret, between the shadow and the soul.

I love you as the plant that never blooms
but carries in itself the light of hidden flowers;
thanks to your love a certain solid fragrance,
risen from the earth, lives darkly in my body.

I love you without knowing how, or when, or from where.
I love you straightforwardly, without complexities or pride;
so I love you because I know no other way
than this: where I do not exist, nor you,
so close that your hand on my chest is my hand,
so close that your eyes close as I fall asleep.

From I LIKE YOU

1965 / SANDOL STODDARD WARBURG

I like you
And I know why
I like you because
You are a good person
To like
I like you because
When I tell you something special
You know it's special
And you remember it
A long long time
You say remember when
you told me
Something special
And both of us remember
When I think something is important
You think it's important too
We have good ideas
When I say something funny
You laugh
I think I'm funny and
You think I'm funny too

. . . .

You really like me

Don't you

And I really like you back

And you like me back

And I like you back

And that's the way we keep on going

Every day

. . . .

On the Fourth of July

I like you because

It's the Fourth of July

On the Fifth of July

I like you too

. . . .

Even if it was the

nine hundred and ninety-

ninth of July

Even if it was

August

Even if it was way down at the bottom of November

Even if it was no place particular in January

I would go on choosing you

And you would

go on choosing me

Over and over again

. . . .

COMING HOME
from DREAM WORK

1986 / MARY OLIVER

When we are driving, in the dark,
on the long road
to Provincetown, which lies empty
for miles, when we are weary,
when the buildings
and the scrub pines lose
their familiar look,
I imagine us rising
from the speeding car,
I imagine us seeing
everything from another place—the top
of one of the pale dunes
or the deep and nameless
fields of the sea—
and what we see is the world
that cannot cherish us
but which we cherish,
and what we see is our life

moving like that,
along the dark edges
of everything—the headlights
like lanterns
sweeping the blackness—
believing in a thousand
fragile and unprovable things,
looking out for sorrow,
slowing down for happiness,
making all the right turns
right down to the thumping
barriers to the sea,
the swirling waves,
the narrow streets, the houses,
the past, the future,
the doorway that belongs
to you and me.

NUPTIALS

2000 / JOHN AGARD

River, be their teacher,
that together they may turn
their future highs and lows
into one hopeful flow

Two opposite shores
feeding from a single source.

Mountain, be their milestone,
that hand in hand they rise above
familiarity's worn tracks
into horizons of their own
Two separate footpaths
dreaming of a common peak.

Birdsong, be their mantra,
that down the frail aisles of their days,
their twilight hearts twitter morning
and their dreams prove branch enough.

From

GOODRIDGE V. DEPARTMENT OF PUBLIC HEALTH

NOVEMBER 18, 2003 / CHIEF JUSTICE MARGARET H. MARSHALL, MASSACHUSETTS SUPREME JUDICIAL COURT

Marriage is a vital social institution. The exclusive commitment of two individuals to each other nurtures love and mutual support; it brings stability to our society. For those who choose to marry, and for their children, marriage provides an abundance of legal, financial, and social benefits. In return it imposes weighty legal, financial, and social obligations . . .

Without question, civil marriage enhances the "welfare of the community." It is a "social institution of the highest importance."* Civil marriage anchors an ordered society by encouraging stable relationships over transient ones . . .

Marriage also bestows enormous private and social advantages on those who choose to marry. Civil marriage is at once a deeply personal commitment to another human being and a highly public celebration of the ideals of mutuality, companionship, intimacy, fidelity, and family. "It is an association that promotes a way of life, not causes; a harmony in living, not political faiths; a bilateral loyalty, not commercial or social projects."** Because it fulfils yearnings for security, safe haven, and connection that express our common humanity, civil marriage is an esteemed institution, and the decision whether and whom to marry is among life's momentous acts of self-definition.

*French v. McAnarney, 290 Mass. 544, 546 (1935)
**Griswold v. Connecticut, 381 US 479, 486 (1965)

From

OBERGEFELL V. HODGES

JUNE 26, 2015 / JUSTICE ANTHONY KENNEDY,
UNITED STATES SUPREME COURT

No union is more profound than marriage, for it embodies
the highest ideals of love, fidelity, devotion, sacrifice, and
family. In forming a marital union, two people become
something greater than once they were. As some of the
petitioners in these cases demonstrate, marriage embod-
ies a love that may endure even past death. It would mis-
understand these men and women to say they disrespect
the idea of marriage. Their plea is that they do respect it,
respect it so deeply that they seek to find its fulfillment for
themselves. Their hope is not to be condemned to live in
loneliness, excluded from one of civilization's oldest institu-
tions. They ask for equal dignity in the eyes of the law. The
Constitution grants them that right.

WEDDING THOUGHTS: ALL I KNOW ABOUT LOVE

2017 / NEIL GAIMAN

This is everything I have to tell you about love: *nothing.*
This is everything I've learned about marriage: *nothing.*

Only that the world out there is complicated,
and there are beasts in the night, and delight and pain,
and the only thing that makes it okay, sometimes,
is to reach out a hand in the darkness and find another
hand to squeeze,
and not to be alone.

It's not the kisses, or never just the kisses: it's what
they mean.
Somebody's got your back.
Somebody knows your worst self and somehow doesn't
want to rescue you
or send for the army to rescue them.

It's not two broken halves becoming one.
It's the light from a distant lighthouse bringing you both
safely home
because home is wherever you are both together.

So this is everything I have to tell you about love and marriage: *nothing,*

like a book without pages or a forest without trees.

Because there are things you cannot know before you experience them.

Because no study can prepare you for the joys or the trials.

Because nobody else's love, nobody else's marriage, is like yours,

and it's a road you can only learn by walking it,

a dance you cannot be taught,

a song that did not exist before you began, together, to sing.

And because in the darkness you will reach out a hand,

not knowing for certain if someone else is even there.

And your hands will meet,

and then neither of you will ever need to be alone again.

And that's all I know about love.

OF WEDDED

2018 / NICOLE COOLEY

Wed, from Old English for *a pledge*.

To be devoted—yes—

yet in my favorite stories why is luck always linked to ruin?

In the Roman Empire, a husband breaks a barley cake over his new bride's head, symbol of fertility.

Remember how I cracked apart frozen pieces of our cake and packed them, brought them to Cambodia to meet you?

Medieval England: spiced buns are piled high and a bride and groom must kiss across the stack without it tumbling to the floor—

I want to be assured—

if the wedded couple does not knock the cake over they are *assured prosperity*.

How to smash and destroy yet still be lucky?

When the cake falls, the wedding guests gather the crumbs into confetti—

once, we slept carefully with pineapple-filled broken slices under our pillow in a Hong Kong hotel

while moonlight rinsed the bed, while we began our marriage.

HOW FALLING IN LOVE IS LIKE OWNING A DOG

2019 / TAYLOR MALI

First of all, it's a big responsibility,
especially in a city like New York.
So think long and hard before deciding on love.
On the other hand, love gives you a sense of security:
when you're walking down the street late at night
and you have a leash on love
ain't no one going to mess with you.
Because crooks and muggers think love is unpredictable.
Who knows what love could do in its own defense?

On cold winter nights, love is warm.
It lies between you and lives and breathes
and makes funny noises.
Love wakes you up all hours of the night with its needs.
It needs to be fed so it will grow and stay healthy.

Love doesn't like being left alone for long.
But come home and love is always happy to see you.
It may break a few things accidentally in its passion for life,
but you can never be mad at love for long.

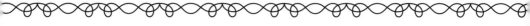

Is love good all the time? No! No!
Love can be bad. Bad, love, bad! Very bad love.

Love makes messes.
Love leaves you little surprises here and there.
Love needs lots of cleaning up after.
Sometimes you just want to get love fixed.
Sometimes you want to roll up a piece of newspaper
and swat love on the nose,
not so much to cause pain,
just to let love know *Don't you ever do that again!*

Sometimes love just wants to go out for a nice long walk.
Because love loves exercise. It will run you around the block
and leave you panting, breathless. Pull you in different directions
at once, or wind itself around and around you
until you're all wound up and you cannot move.

But love makes you meet people wherever you go.
People who have nothing in common but love
stop and talk to each other on the street.

Throw things away and love will bring them back,
again, and again, and again.
But most of all, love needs love, lots of it.
And in return, love loves you and never stops.

BLESSING FOR A MARRIAGE

JAMES DILLET FREEMAN

May your marriage bring you all the exquisite excitements a marriage should bring,

and may life grant you also patience, tolerance, and understanding.

May you always need one another—not so much to fill your emptiness

as to help you to know your fullness.

A mountain needs a valley to be complete;

the valley does not make the mountain less, but more;

and the valley is more a valley

because it has a mountain towering over it.

So let it be with you and you.

May you need one another, but not out of weakness.

May you want one another, but not out of lack.

May you entice one another, but not compel one another.

May you embrace one another, but not encircle one another.

May you succeed in all important ways with one another,

and not fail in the little graces.

May you look for things to praise, often say, "I love you!"

and take no notice of small faults.

If you have quarrels that push you apart,

May both of you hope to have good sense

enough to take the first step back.

May you enter into the mystery which is the awareness of one
another's presence—

no more physical than spiritual, warm and

near when you are side by side, and warm

and near when you are in separate rooms

or even distant cities.

May you have happiness, and may you

find it making one another happy.

May you have love, and may you find it

loving one another!

BLESSING OF THE HANDS

REVEREND DANIEL L. HARRIS

These are the hands of your best friend, young and strong and full of love for you, that are holding yours on your wedding day, as you promise to love each other today, tomorrow, and forever.

These are the hands that will work alongside yours, as together you build your future.

These are the hands that will passionately love you and cherish you through the years, and with the slightest touch, will comfort you like no other.

These are the hands that will hold you when fear or grief fills your mind.

These are the hands that will countless times wipe the tears from your eyes; tears of sorrow, and tears of joy.

These are the hands that will tenderly hold your children.

These are the hands that will help you to hold your family as one.

These are the hands that will give you strength when you need it.

And lastly, these are the hands that even when wrinkled and aged, will still be reaching for yours, still giving you the same unspoken tenderness with just a touch.

A BLESSING FOR THE JOURNEY

ROSHI WENDY EGYOKU NAKAO

Let us vow to bear witness to the wholeness of life,
realizing the completeness of each and every thing.
Embracing our differences,
I shall know myself as you,
and you as myself.
May we serve each other
for all our days,
here, there, and everywhere.
Let us vow to open ourselves to the abundance of life.
Freely giving and receiving, I shall care for you,
for the trees and stars,
as treasures of my very own.
May we be grateful
for all our days,
here, there, and everywhere.
Let us vow to forgive all hurt,
caused by ourselves and others,
and to never condone hurtful ways.
Being responsible for my actions,
I shall free myself and you.
Will you free me, too?

May we be kind

for all our days,

here, there, and everywhere.

Let us vow to remember that all that appears
will disappear.

In the midst of uncertainty,

I shall sow love.

Here! Now! I call to you:

Let us together live

The Great Peace that we are.

May we give no fear

for all our days,

here, there, and everywhere.

TRADITIONAL IRISH BLESSING

May the road rise to meet you,
May the wind be always at your back.
May the sun shine warm upon your face,
The rains fall soft upon your fields.
And until we meet again,
May God hold you in the palm of his hand.

May God be with you and bless you;
May you see your children's children.
May you be poor in misfortune,
Rich in blessings,
May you know nothing but happiness
From this day forward.

May the road rise to meet you
May the wind be always at your back.
May the warm rays of sun fall upon your home
And may the hand of a friend always be near.

May green be the grass you walk on,
May blue be the skies above you,
May pure be the joys that surround you,
May true be the hearts that love you.

CHEROKEE PRAYER

God in heaven above please protect the ones we love.

We honor all you created as we pledge our hearts and lives together.

We honor Mother Earth and ask for our marriage to be abundant and grow stronger through the seasons;

We honor fire and ask that our union be warm and glowing with love in our hearts;

We honor wind and ask that we sail through life safe and calm as in our father's arms;

We honor water to clean and soothe our relationship that it may never thirst for love;

With all the forces of the universe you created, we pray for harmony and true happiness as we forever grow young together. Aho.

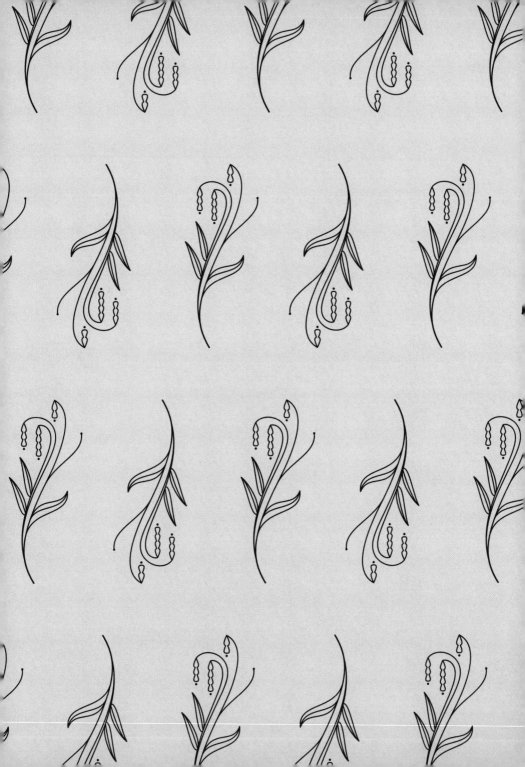

THE BUDDHA'S SERMON AT RAJAGAHA, VERSES 19–20

Do not deceive, do not despise
each other anywhere.
Do not be angry nor
bear secret resentments;
for as a mother will risk her life
and watches over her child,
so boundless be your love to all,
so tender, kind and mild.

Cherish good will right and left,
early and late,
and without hindrance, without stint,
be free of hate and envy,
while standing and walking and sitting down,
whatever you have in mind,
the rule of life that is always best
is to be loving and kind.

BUDDHIST MARRIAGE HOMILY

Nothing happens without a cause. The union of this man and woman has not come about accidentally but is the foreordained result of many past lives. This tie can therefore not be broken or dissolved.

In the future, happy occasions will come as surely as the morning. Difficult times will come as surely as the night. When things go joyously, meditate according to the Buddhist tradition. When things go badly, meditate. Meditation in the manner of Compassionate Buddha will guide your life.

To say the words "love and compassion" is easy. But to accept that love and compassion are built upon patience and perseverance is not easy. Your marriage will be firm and lasting if you remember this.

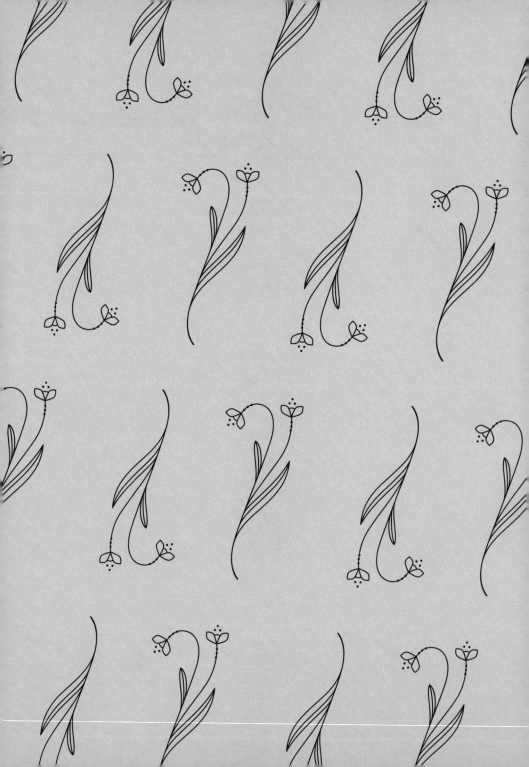

From
THE ART OF POWER

2007 / THICH NHAT HANH

The Buddha spoke about four elements that constitute true love: the capacity to be kind and offer happiness, *maitri* in Sanskrit; compassion, the capacity to relieve suffering, *karuna;* the capacity to bring joy every day, *mudita;* and finally, the capacity of nondiscrimination, *upeksha.* When there is true love, there is nondiscrimination. The pain of the other is our own pain; the happiness of the other is our own happiness . . .

To make our love meaningful, we need to nourish our *bodhicitta,* our mind of boundless love and compassion . . .

First, we learn to love one person with all our understanding and insight; then we expand that love to embrace another person, and another, until our love is truly boundless.

ECCLESIASTES 4:9–12

(NEW INTERNATIONAL VERSION)

Two are better than one,
    because they have a good return for their labor:
If either of them falls down,
    one can help the other up.
But pity anyone who falls
    and has no one to help them up.
Also, if two lie down together, they will keep warm.
    But how can one keep warm alone?
Though one may be overpowered,
    two can defend themselves.
A cord of three strands is not quickly broken.

COLOSSIANS 3:12-17

(NEW INTERNATIONAL VERSION)

Therefore, as God's chosen people, holy and dearly loved, clothe yourselves with compassion, kindness, humility, gentleness and patience. Bear with each other and forgive one another if any of you has a grievance against someone. Forgive as the Lord forgave you. And over all these virtues put on love, which binds them all together in perfect unity.

Let the peace of Christ rule in your hearts, since as members of one body you were called to peace. And be thankful. Let the message of Christ dwell among you richly as you teach and admonish one another with all wisdom through psalms, hymns, and songs from the Spirit, singing to God with gratitude in your hearts. And whatever you do, whether in word or deed, do it all in the name of the Lord Jesus, giving thanks to God the Father through him.

1 CORINTHIANS 13

(NEW INTERNATIONAL VERSION)

If I speak in the tongues of men or of angels, but do not have love, I am only a resounding gong or a clanging cymbal. If I have the gift of prophecy and can fathom all mysteries and all knowledge, and if I have a faith that can move mountains, but do not have love, I am nothing. If I give all I possess to the poor and give over my body to hardship that I may boast, but do not have love, I gain nothing.

Love is patient, love is kind. It does not envy, it does not boast, it is not proud. It does not dishonor others, it is not self-seeking, it is not easily angered, it keeps no record of wrongs. Love does not delight in evil but rejoices with the truth. It always protects, always trusts, always hopes, always perseveres.

Love never fails. But where there are prophecies, they will cease; where there are tongues, they will be stilled; where there is knowledge, it will pass away. For we know in part and we prophesy in part, but when completeness comes, what is in part disappears. When I was a child, I talked like a child, I thought like a child, I reasoned like a child. When I became a man, I put the ways of childhood behind me. For now we see only a reflection as in a mirror; then we shall see face to face. Now I know in part; then I shall know fully, even as I am fully known.

And now these three remain: faith, hope and love. But the greatest of these is love.

HINDU MARRIAGE POEM

You have become mine forever.

Yes, we have become partners.

I have become yours.

Hereafter, I cannot live without you.

Do not live without me.

Let us share the joys.

We are word and meaning, united.

You are thought and I am sound.

May the nights be honey-sweet for us.

May the mornings be honey-sweet for us.

May the plants be honey-sweet for us.

May the earth be honey-sweet for us.

A HINDU LOVE POEM

Let the earth of my body be mixed with the earth
my beloved walks on.

Let the fire of my body be the brightness
in the mirror that reflects his face.

Let the water of my body join the waters
of the lotus pool he bathes in.

Let the breath of my body be air
lapping his tired limbs.

Let me be sky, and moving through me the
cloud-dark Shyama, my beloved.

SAPTAPADI
(SEVEN STEPS)

Let us take the first step to provide for our household a nourishing and pure diet, avoiding those foods injurious to healthy living.

Let us take the second step to develop physical, mental, and spiritual powers.

Let us take the third step to increase our wealth by righteous means and proper use.

Let us take the fourth step to acquire knowledge, happiness, and harmony by mutual love and trust.

Let us take the fifth step so that we are blessed with strong, virtuous, and heroic children.

Let us take the sixth step for self-restraint and longevity.

Finally, let us take the seventh step and be true companions and remain lifelong partners by this marriage.

SONG OF SONGS (OR SONG OF SOLOMON) 2:10–14

My beloved speaks and says to me:

Arise, my love, my fair one, and come away;

for lo, the winter is past, the rain is over and gone.

The flowers appear on the earth, the time of singing has come, and the voice of the turtle-dove is heard in our land.

The fig tree ripens her green figs, and the vines are in blossom; they give forth fragrance.

Arise, my love, my fair one, and come away.

O my dove, in the clefts of the rock, in the covert of the cliff,

let me see your face, let me hear your voice, for your voice is sweet, and your face is lovely.

From
RUTH 1:16–17

IN THE TALMUD

But Ruth replied, "Don't urge me to leave you or to turn back from you. Where you go I will go, and where you stay I will stay. Your people will be my people and your God my God. Where you die I will die, and there I will be buried. May the Lord deal with me, be it ever so severely, if even death separates you and me."

THE SEVEN BENEDICTIONS (SHEVA BRACHOT)

Blessed art Thou, O lord our God, King of the Universe who has created the fruit of the vine.

Blessed art Thou, O lord our God, King of the Universe who has created all things for His glory.

Blessed art Thou, O lord our God, King of the Universe, creator of man.

Blessed art Thou, O lord our God, King of the Universe who has made man in his image, after his likeness, and has prepared for him, out of his very self, a perpetual fabric. Blessed art Thou, O Lord, creator of man.

May she who was barren be exceedingly glad and rejoice when her children are united in her midst in joy. Blessed art Thou, O Lord, who makes Zion joyful through her children.

O Lord, make these beloved companions greatly rejoice even as Thou did rejoice at Thy creation in the Garden of Eden as of old. Blessed art Thou, O Lord, who makes bridegroom and bride to rejoice.

Blessed art Thou, O lord our God, King of the Universe, who has created joy and gladness, bridegroom and bride, mirth and exultation, pleasure and delight, love, brotherhood, peace and fellowship. Soon may there be heard in the cities of Judah and in the streets of Jerusalem, the voice of joy and gladness, the voice of the bridegroom and the voice of the bride, the jubilant voice of the bridegrooms from the canopies, and of youths from their feasts of song. Blessed art Thou, O Lord who makes the bridegroom to rejoice with the bride.

From
AL-FATIHA
(THE OPENING)

IN THE QUR'AN

In the name of God, the infinitely Compassionate and Merciful.

Praise be to God, Lord of all the worlds. The Compassionate, the Merciful. Ruler on the Day of Reckoning.

You alone do we worship, and You alone do we ask for help.

Guide us on the straight path, the path of those who have received your grace; not the path of those who have brought down wrath, nor of those who wander astray. Amen.

QUR'AN 4:1, 3:102, 33:70-71

O mankind, fear your Lord, who created you from one soul and created from it its mate and dispersed from both of them many men and women. And fear Allah, through whom you ask one another, and the wombs. Indeed Allah is ever, over you, an Observer.

O you who have believed, fear Allah as He should be feared and do not die except as Muslims [in submission to Him].

O you who have believed, fear Allah and speak words of appropriate justice. He will [then] amend for you your deeds and forgive you your sins. And whoever obeys Allah and His Messenger has certainly attained a great attainment.

QUR'AN 30:21

And of His signs is that He created for you from
yourselves mates that you may find tranquility in
them; and He placed between you affection and
mercy. Indeed in that are signs for a people who
give thought.

ADDITIONAL RESOURCES

In addition to the fifty readings in this collection, there are endless resources to help you find the perfect words for your wedding. We listed more of our favorites below.

POEMS AND BLESSINGS

Maya Angelou, "Touched by an Angel"

John Ciardi, "Most Like an Arch This Marriage"

John Cooper Clarke, "I Wanna Be Yours"

Roy Croft, "Love"

Louise Cuddon, "I'll Be There for You"

Robert Frost, "Master Speed"

Robert Fulghum, "Union"

Neil Gaiman, "This Is for You"

Rupi Kaur, "I Do Not Want to Have You"

James Kavanaugh, "To Love Is Not to Possess"

Pablo Neruda, "Sonnet XLIII"

Edmund O'Neil, "Marriage Joins Two People in the Circle of Its Love"

BOOKS

Do a quick search for any of these titles + "wedding reading" for applicable passages.

Richard Bach, *The Bridge Across Forever*

Paulo Coelho, *The Alchemist*

Louis de Bernières, *Corelli's Mandolin*

John Green, *The Fault in Our Stars*

Ernest Hemingway, *A Farewell to Arms*

Lang Leav, *Love & Misadventure*

Madeleine L'Engle, *The Irrational Season*

Cormac McCarthy, *The Road*

A. A. Milne, *Winnie the Pooh*

Boris Pasternak, *Doctor Zhivago*

Philip Pullman, *The Amber Spyglass*

Tom Robbins, *Still Life with Woodpecker*

Hilary T. Smith, *Wild Awake*

SONGS

Sara Bareilles, "I Choose You"

Leonard Cohen, "Dance Me to the End of Love"

Roberta Flack, "The First Time Ever I Saw Your Face"

Led Zeppelin, "Thank You"

Justin Timberlake, "Mirrors"

The Velvet Underground, "I'll Be Your Mirror"

Stevie Wonder, "You Are the Sunshine of My Life"

MOVIES

Do a quick search for any of these titles + "wedding reading" for applicable quotes.

10 Things I Hate About You

Carol

Dirty Dancing

Love Actually

Notting Hill

Shakespeare in Love

Silver Linings Playbook

Titanic

West Side Story

When Harry Met Sally

CREDITS